Letters From a Quiet Coast

Michelle Bauer

BookLeaf Publishing

Presentation by *BookLeaf Publishing*

Web: www.bookleafpub.com

E-mail: info@bookleafpub.com

ISBN: 978-93-95755-43-6

First edition 2022

To my grandmother, for her love of sunshine.

To my parents, for their want of the stars.

This is for you.

PREFACE

In the beginning, there was Icarus,
parting the clouds with his palms
and splitting the thunder with his laughter.

In the end, there was Icarus,
falling through the sky,
and floating in a sea of feathers.

The tragedy was a prophecy
And all who bore witness could only stare.

His tale remains true:
There are those of us who plummet after
unheeded warnings
and those who watch them fall.

Ides of January

Do I know who I am?
It's not February
anymore.

The cat curls on the pillow
purring softly
she looks warm.

The wind taps against the window
quietly, just enough to know
that the clouds are heavy with rain.

It's not February
is it?

The clock on the dresser
it looks foreign with the dust
the little bell that it has

you'd press.

The house seems
well,
empty.

Like most of the space

on the page that I can't fill.

The sheets feel warm and smooth
against my skin
and I feel the inside of my lips
with my tongue.

Perhaps it was
a sweet, sweet dream
that wasn't mine.

never mine.

I still recall the whistle
of the train and the smoke
as it exhaled into the foggy air
that suffocated us at night

You coughed
I laughed

Your eyes looked different
they searched for –
I'm not sure
I ever knew.

Who was I to you?

Forlorn, I may have been from

a book you read
or an old song you sang when you travelled to
the lost city across the sea.

Yes. I think so.

I remember seeing you
on one of the street corners
in a crowd of people that all looked like lights
floating in the sky.

Ok. You're right.

But that was February and it isn't February
anymore
is it?

Stay Here in the Golden Sun

I think of how you look
silhouetted, your fingers to your forehead
squinting your eyes as you look out
at the old city
painted red and gold in the setting sunlight.

You notice me looking
and smile tenderly.

These are the moments I will remember you in
long after you are gone:

Happy and calm
the gentleness of your soul
welcoming the world towards you -
you are magnificent,
love personified.

I think of all the artists
in past lives
who would have formed you
just like one of their figures
with your arm thrown above your head
in the twisted sheets
your lips parted just enough

for viewers to think they are not staged.

I think of the warmth in your eyes
as they dance and twirl when you look at me
and I can see it all:
everything you've become.

I see you gazing beyond
the walls of the old city
and I know
that when you go
you will take a part of my heart with you.

I think I've always known.

And I am fraid
I will never see you
the way that I have today.

To Achilles, to Cleopatra,
to all the love-stricken kings and queens
of myth and legend:
Please. Do not go.

Stay here in the golden sun
with me
where we are happy
and I'll love you 'till forever comes.

A Quiet Winter

I did not know it would take old age
for me to notice
the veins on leaves
as the winter winds bite
at the flowers and their stems.

I loved you
as you screamed at me
from across the kitchen
barefoot on tile
throwing your hands in the air
still wet from the sink water.

I loved you with
a heart on fire
a bitter
tender
lust
when you cried
that I could never love someone
so fragile.

We were both fragile
darling

We were both waiting
for the thunder outside to calm
and for the sky to open up
and swallow us whole.

Could you not see it then?
The way the darkness loomed
an empty presence
a forbidden guest
sitting quietly at a table
it was never invited to.

I knew I loved you
the morning I found you
it could have been anywhere
darling.

You'd tense up
furrow your brow
and tell me about the awfulness
of a day that seemed beautiful.
And I knew then.

So you see
As you go
just know
it has not been without love
that we have ached and longed
and run wild in circles in forests

so thick we cannot see the sun
through the veins of the leaves.

Ink

Here's my confession:
I don't know if I'm doing it right.

I sit with ink on my
chapped palms against soft
wood of a desk so old
I am swimming through
the forest so ancient
it stretches to the sea

and the world is just me
and the ink on my palms.

And all I can think of is the pillow
against the cold skin of my face
and the moonlight I wanted
to drape me and fill me with wonder
as the porch door swung against
the frame and the emptiness
lingered in the room like the stars
had fallen from beyond
the window and in the distance
a small silhouette appeared of you

and the night felt so dreadfully lonely

so the morning would, too.

In the absence I write
with ink on my palms

The stories of the night and the stars

Here is my confession:
I don't know if I'm doing it right.

Words

I asked myself
if there were words for what I was feeling.

There were none.

Just you and me
in a small room
looking at each other
when the other looks away.

I Think of You

I wonder if you know I think of you
when the summer winds blow
and the air smells like early Autumn
like camp fires that have yet to darken.

When the grass is filled with dew
beneath our feet and the willow leaves fall
and the sky is clear enough to show all
I think of you.

I think of you
when the flowers bloom and
our salt-tipped fingers dip in deep
to the bowl on the picnic table.

When the beach sands feel warm enough
for us to lay upon with puffed out chests
ready to breathe deep and let go
of the weight of the world.

I think of you
during star-glazed nights
when the moon hangs low enough to trace
with our hopeful gaze and clasped palms.

When the morning birds sing
from their branches lakeside, calling
to one another, like we did through
the hollow tunnels we made with our hands.

I think of you
when my eyes feel burned
from the salt of my tears in the lonely times
and I remember we made it through together.

When the new day arrives and I know
you're there, in the world somewhere
and a small smile widens my cheeks
knowing you exist with me in this dream.

I think of you
when the end of the day nears
and I rid my mind of fears
because of you,

that's when I think of you.

Rain

I was rain
I was a lot of things
all at once;
but most of me was rain
falling down
and down
and down
until I was nothing more than parts of myself
sprawled on the ashen pavement
of the city streets
disassembled in the orange haze
of lamp post lighting
and still
I was more myself
as nothing you could see
than I was when you thought
I came from the sky.

Fire Bird

There were many ways I knew her

golden skin and fire hair

angel wings tucked in tightly -
too tightly, she wouldn't fly away.

In these small moments, I miss her.

Not who she was to me,
but who she used to be for herself
in all those in-between places she let herself
wander; where did she go to, I wonder?

I miss her quiet ways. The small smile
she'd give
from behind the rim of the coffee mug
late night jazz and smoke filled rooms
pressing shadows against the sides of her lips.

I wonder if those places
miss her too? Like I do. Like maybe
they miss her presence and the way she occupied
them all, sitting crossed legged at wooden
tables, checking the cracks

in the pink polish coating her nails.

I suppose in a way this is my love song to her.
This pain of remembering. For what love is
more profound that feeling pain for someone
else?

Her shoulders were bare; opened dress
she felt freer than I ever did

And perhaps that was the agony of watching her
soar
far beyond my grasp:
If someone so indestructible could disappear
in the subtle light of a match box flame
then who I am to the world but a ghost?

She was radiance and intense belonging;
and I, like a crippled bird
was cowering beneath her wings.

Now, the sky
the sky
is falling
and it is a beautiful comet.

And she is there;
twirling, evaporating
like thin air and star shine

creating magic as she goes

And she will come back
come back
to me
to us all
a pheonix in her prime.

There were many ways I knew her
will they matter when she is reborn?

The Many Forms of Grief

"It is beautiful out today"

"Yes, I know"

"I was visiting people yesterday"

The tea kettle sits boiling on the counter top
faces near, those we love
the sound of laughter from a different room
one close by
a hidden smile as a mug is chosen
the sun shines through the blinds, scattering
on the surface of the table
sparkling against the creases in the brown oak
like small diamonds
summer dresses hanging loosely
against slender frames, the slight breeze
lifting the hems
the business of a kitchen.

"Wait, I need a minute. Was I visiting people
yesterday?"

A minute passes.

"No, I don't think I was"

"No, you never left"

"Oh"

And grief comes
in the tender sigh
at the end of a word.

From the First Square

I was the knight and you were the pawn
and I could only watch your sacrifice
as I readied myself for battle;

Knowing, as your figure fell
victory would be unforgiving.

When I Say I Love You

When I say I love you
I do not mean I would buy you
pretty gifts with bows and string;

I do not mean I would tuck you in
at night and kiss your cheek

I do not mean I would call you
to see if you are feeling better
after your illness;

I mean I would plummet into the depths
of a dark tide to find you
as the water fills my lungs and the salt
stings my eyes, I would fight
until I reached you and I would drag you
to shore

I mean if ghosts were real
flesh and bone, I would battle
every one that held you from me
until my knuckles bled

I mean that you mean as much as air
and I would search the cave for hours

days
years
until your return

When I say I love you
I mean you can trust me with your soul
because ours are intertwined.

Porch Doors

I remembered you
every day
for lifetimes

I sat in
shallow tides
and let them
sooth my skin

And still;
you lingered
all around
like the summer air

We breathed you in
and let you go

And just like summer
you were
hurricanes and wildfire

Sable hair
on a porch swing
swaying

Lamp light under
a moonlit
sky

A gentle surrender
of the clock
to the moment

Denim jackets
at the back of the bar
with the lights low

We laughed louder than
the record playing
in the next room

The summer heat
left us burning
sitting on the front step

And you smiled
like I had forever
to smile back

Until one night
with the porch door closing
just like summer
you were gone.

The World

I hope my children know
the earth was once beautiful
it held rainforests and cups of warm tea on
cloudy days
fresh pancakes with loved ones
with blueberries in the middle
we sang to each other
sweet lullabys and grand operas
performed open heart surgeries
to continue supporting the lives we could
I hope they know at night we watched the stars
shine
we sat on thin fabric blankets in cut grass
and pointed at the sky together
we turned the worn pages of old books
that we kept near the fireplace in the library
in the dark, we touched the palms of those we
loved
to find the creases and stains and to paint
the outline of skin into our minds
some of us prayed and others hoped
but it was all very beautiful
I hope they know that that was our world
wrinkled smiles and late night laughs

small birds in the forest speaking from their
branches
to the other woodland creatures
and I hope they know that's why we fought
to find our world again
to give them it
not this
not this.

Sinking Sands

These sinking sands
they pull me

Until I am
no more

A wave, a taste
the bitterness of sea

I have seen you in the small moments;
lost time and reverie
small glasses of something sweet at night
as I lift my legs to the table for rest

The record is on the table
it's played too many times
but you keep saying the night is young
the cool air comes in through a balcony door

These sinking sands pull me
sleep-filled eyes and pillow lips

Remember my skin, my bones, my whispers

For these pulling sands are taking me deeper
and they disappeared so long
long ago.

A Gentle Song

I'm sorry you lost
a part of you;

It chipped away
that fateful day.

Lost in
mountains gray;
long grass sway
midnight sun.

You opened your eyes and -
they were gone.

Were they ever
really there?

Wrinkled smiles in
the car at night
the stars filled
their eyes

Reflected the sky
laughs and cold breath
dim hotel lights

in the foreground.

The water runs
up and down the mountain
up and down
they shiver.

You blinked and
you were alone
the passenger seat empty
still warm.

Now you walk this
ancient isle
feeling it in your skin:
the memory of
what once was.

I'm sorry you lost
a part of you,
you feel it now -
a form of surrender.

Your breathing quickens
your hands are bare
the tender heart yearns
for more.

For now, remember

the words you shared
and sing
your gentle song.

Of mountains gray
of long grass
of the part that
chipped away.

Slumber

Feelings of hollow
trees that grow
branches breaking
trampled snow

Far beneath the sulking willow
leaves green vine; armor
roots thick and gripping ground
try not to make a sound

Twisting, turning
firelight yearning
feelings sorrow still;
pen and quill

These years are ending quickly
sleep well, for slumber is the key
to quench this gentle yearning
attempt to close your eyes

Forbidden lies, always dreary
follow your heart, never astray
fade away, then come back
become what you were before
slumber.

Wither

Maybe I didn't say it loud enough
or stretch my bones
soften my skin
enough
to fly away
but let me say it now
loudly
clearly
boldly
confidently:

I will not wither.

You were firelight
 in a storm
 and the woods were quieted for your thunder
 for your flashes of light and fury
 as you wet the leaves and bent their roots
 as you raged at the clouds and
 beat at the soil

But the petals did not fall
the creeks welcomed you in
let their waters overflow
until they drowned

out your noise

And the whispers from the mountains
called back to you
for more
and like their stones
haunted and aged

You howled

Your tears, as raindrops
fell to the earth
lost to the chaos
you created

You left behind

these woods cannot forget you
these woods cannot forgive you

Your ghost still lingers
here
for all to feel

I wish you could see
the aftermath of your
destruction

The quiet serenity

that came
in the moments after
as the soul of the forest healed
and grew
and learned again
how to stretch to the sky -
it was beautiful to see:

The rebirth.

I hope, in your shadowed journey
you find
your voice has quieted
the rage you knew so well, contemplative
instead
a solitude unbound
for you to choose
as you plod before the fields
upon them, with them, through them
I hope over the peaks of the white-caps
of the songbirds waiting
you hear it:

I did not wither.

Angry Waters

Angry water
angry water
why are you angered so?

You tilt my boat
my small, frail boat
as I gently sail to shore

The sun is warm
the day is starting
why are you angered so?

Angry water
angry water
why can't the sea stay calm

Your majesty
when tides are still
it beckons every sailor

You need not swell
nor spray the air
instead, take rest out yonder

Angry water

angry water
you frighten me like this

On quieter days
you let me slumber
resting well in peace

On days like today
instead, you roar
your mighty waves still grow

Angry water
angry water

Why are
you angered
so?

Sinking City

I wonder if you sense the world is moving
the heavy waves lift the cement beneath us
ushering in the new earth
the solstice hangs beneath the clouds
vibrancy fills the land
soft touches I wish I'd known sooner
legacies in the wind, pushing
and in the horizon they walk with baited
breathes
step by step
learning to walk
aren't we all
in the chilled mid December chaotic winds

I am so cold
the bridge before me towers over the water
I've seen its path lit at nightfall
glowing through the fog
a beacon to the wanderers who plod
a noble path to somewhere else
and the gulls call to one another in frustration
pecking at the tides
the people stop to stare
at the creatures who flutter beyond them

I am saddened by the voice I need
it is angry and grows angrier still
the waves crash and I drown
beneath the cement concaved walls
the floor gives in
sinking
and I in this city of sin
sink with it.

Free

In the sea salt
sand dusted petals
lightly
air
I have breathed you

Like snowfall in the mountains
you have covered the ground

And the vapors rise from hot streams
as they empty into shallow pools
but the sun burns the ice
it burns right through

And I sit and watch you dance
in black sand

You are wild in this place
and we have never been so free

I return here often in my mind
freckled skin from a mid October sun
and the air is cold I know
but I did not bring a blanket

Instead I dip my toe in
letting the tiny ripple it creates flow away
and then
I sink my feet in
to the murky depths I cannot see

Will you wait for me
will I wait for me
in the meadow at midnight when the horizon
is still ablaze and the creatures
who roam and play in green grass
sing to one another.

Oh, the sea salt
Are you free
Are you free
Are you gone?

Sketchbook

In the sketchbook in the cupboard
the pages are all emoty
the memory of your hands
brings back the outline
and I suppose that's key
lightly, you'd say
taking the pen
pressing it to the page
and then biting your lip.
I miss the figurines you'd draw
all those lovely faces row by row
it was never me
I broke too easy
try to keep it, I think
rip the pages
throw them down
I remember the vibrant reds of the curtain
behind your fragile frame
as you raised your voice and your mouth
became wide and your eyes looked
a million years older
the words you said were wise
all I ever did was hold you
I could never sing your tune
the way you needed

and I think of all those empty pages
and I think of all those empty words
and I wonder when you draw again
what the figure will look like
me
or
her?

www.ingramcontent.com/pod-product-compliance
Lightning Source LLC
LaVergne TN
LVHW021306200726
843509LV00012B/1816